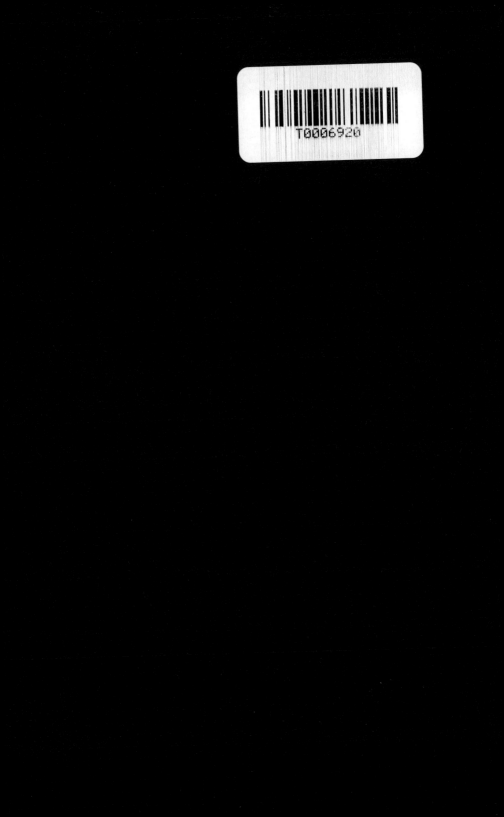

PEONY VERTIGO

Also by Jan Conn

Tomorrow's Bright White Light
Edge Effects
Botero's Beautiful Horses
Jaguar Rain
Beauties on Mad River
What Dante Did with Loss
South of the Tudo Bem Café
The Fabulous Disguise of Ourselves
Red Shoes in the Rain

With Mary di Michele, Susan Gillis, and Jane Munro
(Yoko's Dogs)
Caution Tape
Rhinoceros
Whisk

PEONY
VERTIGO

JAN CONN

Brick Books

Library and Archives Canada Cataloguing in Publication

Title: Peony vertigo / Jan Conn.
Names: Conn, Jan E., author.
Description: Poems.
Identifiers: Canadiana (print) 20230465374 | Canadiana (ebook) 20230465390 |
ISBN 9781771316163 (softcover) | ISBN 9781771316187 (PDF) |
ISBN 9781771316170 (EPUB)
Classification: LCC PS8555 O543 P46 2023 | DDC C811/.54—dc23

Copyright © Jan Conn, 2023

We gratefully acknowledge the Canada Council for the Arts, the Government of Canada
through the Canada Book Fund, and the Ontario Arts Council for their support of our
publishing program.

 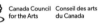

Edited by Sonnet L'Abbé.
Cover painting: "Once on Sado Island," 2022, Jan Conn, acrylic gouache, pencil and acrylic
pen on wood panel.
Author photo kindly provided by Diane M. Conn.
The book is set in Fournier.
Design by Marijke Friesen.
Printed and bound by Coach House Printing.

Brick Books
487 King St. W.
Kingston, ON
K7L 2X7
www.brickbooks.ca

Though much of the work of Brick Books takes place on the ancestral lands of the
Anishinaabeg, Haudenosaunee, Huron-Wendat, and Mississaugas of the Credit peoples, our
editors, authors, and readers from many backgrounds are situated from coast to coast to
coast in Canada on the traditional and unceded territories of over six hundred nations who
have cared for Turtle Island from time immemorial. While living and working on these lands,
we are committed to hearing and returning the rightful imaginative space to the poetries,
songs, and stories that have been untold, under-told, wrongly told, and suppressed through
colonization.

For Carlo

In memory of my brother-in-law Mace Neufeld

In memory of ecologist, collaborator, and friend
Leonardo Suveges Moreira Chaves

CONTENTS

... nous voulons toujours voir ce qui est caché
par ce que nous voyons

René Magritte

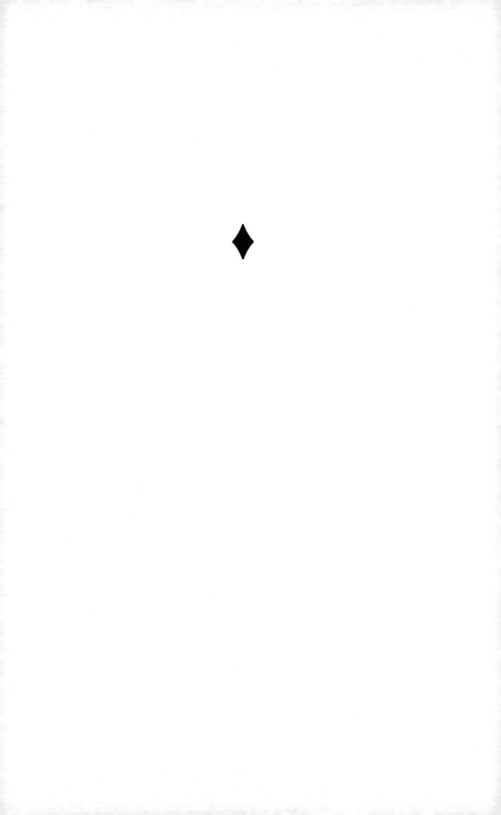

EARLY NOVEMBER

Autumn elbows the windows

Leaving a russet smudge

I slipped in everywhere when I was a woman of fog

Around the corner from the scheme, a green dream

    Around the corner the bird feeders on steroids—
half birdseed, half cayenne pepper, surprise for the bear

Now that I'm here I've forgotten what it was I've always wanted

+++

    The birch tree and its flaming yellow leaves, someone's private life
        on view across the meadow

Along with the washing on the line

Unseasonably hot November days, cedar waxwings high in the hemlocks

Clippers dangling, my sweetheart contemplates the sumacs
        overtaking the yard

Then the midday sky where three exit doors, clearly marked,
        open onto a rainy street

Out of the blue and into the black

+++

Smoky green water surges along the creek bed

Once we identified seven species of goldenrod at the forest edge

Once we sprang a leak

    Now we feel warmer in the kitchen with its brick-red floor tiles

If I could return to my hometown, climb the lookout tower,
      gaze 2000 metres down into the silver crater

    Would I see my father

As I like best to imagine him, waiting for my mother's spirit
    to appear beside him among the river birch

+++

Dashed lines, a crowd of cloudlets, blue jays hip-hopping
    among black cherry and maple branches

On the back porch we painted blue, an Opiliones slowly devours a
    katydid—

I watch from the ringside seat of my hammock

Later the temperature drops, there's grey rain, black ice
    on the slate steps

Flies appear on the windowpanes, drop from the blinds,
        little dots of noir untethered from the day

    In a mural on a building in Lima, a dump truck drives
around and down the narrowing spiral of a miner's heart

+++

By afternoon light I read Su Tung-p'o, view mountain streams

        Meanwhile a red-bellied woodpecker visits, chowing down the
            suet

Meanwhile more holes in the ozone and in a dream
        the landscape assembles: a stained white radiance
barely visible through the oaks

Oaks governed by Jupiter, according to *Culpepper's Herbal*

+++

In my parents' room I rip away the wallpaper, releasing voices—
        my mother singing, a lifetime ago

        Unbidden image of her kneeling in the garden, shears
in hand, delirious pink of peonies

Or in her nursing whites at Toronto General before we were
    formally introduced

I flip a switch and the witch hazel lights up, a subtle
    soothing citron

    Makes me wonder wherefore the hazel, whether the pliability
of those branches is transferrable

Whether the afternoon could be reduced to a fine white powder
    or a flock of juncos

    If the evening becomes coniferous
        and blue as a kingfisher

    If I am a life-size paper doll named Pamela who unfolds
like an accordion

A pine cone in one hand an insect net in the other

+++

A late firefly flashes in the ironwood, the motherboard takes a coffee
    break

    Wind picking up, track lights humming, here comes the solstice

Right when there's an overload of wasp nests in the canopy

A party of voles celebrating their discovery of *Tulipa* and *Crocus*
    Galanthus and *Allium* bulbs

After a slight hitch in the space-time continuum

An effervescence between the indoor palm
  and the red-chili-pepper lights

The afternoon reappears in a tube of cadmium yellow

Accompanying hillside hums continuously where it meets the skyline

  Borders of evergreens and flickering shadows

  To whom shall I reveal my horoscope?

What are my options now that permafrost is not a thing?

  Are there more decades to be found?

To whom shall I address my questions?

+++

The rabbits escaped their hutch and won't be coming back

Light snow and static on the radio, a hike along Charcoal Trail
  more up than down, more white oak than beech

A zigzag in the day, and I step right into it

  The great void, the mystery, the song of the white-throated
    sparrow

Tucking in the iris beds and the creeping dogwood

Oak leaves like polished leather stacked up against the dawn redwood

If we construct a willow house in the understory

If the wind gathers, and the smoke clears

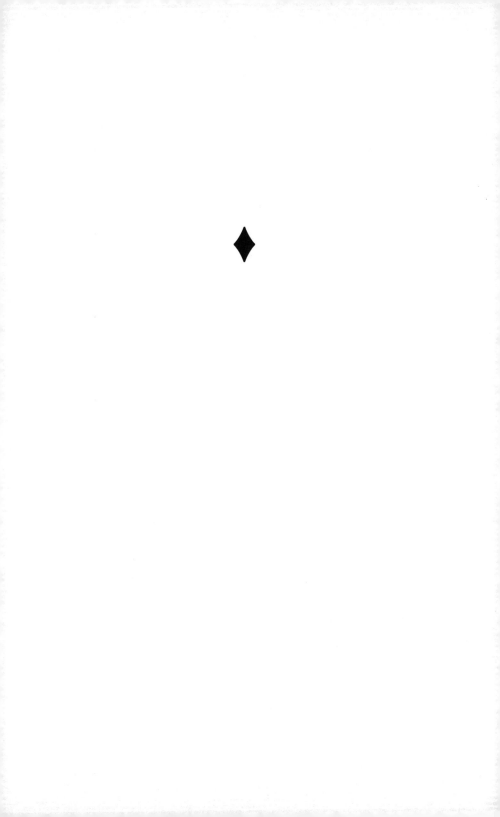

LASCAUX

Leaning hard into a former self, a
borderline sensation
cleaning my psychic house

I open the skylight of my mind
when there's a day moon and the dense
scent of lavender

And then

+++

You aren't from the plains, are you

     The mistral here is harsh and unyielding

Phantoms linger in their borrowed shoes

      Leaves are frightened into falling from their trees

At the entrance to the first cave I slip inside the outline
     of a *cheval*, dun-coloured, shaggy

Darkness is tar-thick, laced with veins nearer to black
than blue, moist as a first-born, far out
        on the scale of anguish

A fissure appears where I discover an extinct
shade of yellow, and charcoal markings, indistinct

As though the past were falling
farther backward as I move toward it

What does a horse vision stand-in for
when life is a blizzard of one

We retain all the lives we've lost ergo
I must have been a prehistoric horse

The logic of my brain these days
beyond reproach, impeccable

I lie on top of the shape my horse takes

Together we speed across the grasslands of the Dordogne
my horse and I

+++

The painter who drew me
ghosts down from the overworld
a horsetail too late
        to follow
        into the inscrutable dark

I left my mane behind
when we flew east

Did I choose the artist?

My herd, invisible, invincible, surrounds
and enfolds me

+++

One by one we gallop away, then wheel to take positions
in the cave's dank embrace

Hidden in the smoky air, feeble torchlight
shivering
mingled scents of herbs and reindeer fat

Horse meat not yet a gourmet dish

Atmosphere a bit tense as the artist
smudges a haunch

Oh ochre, I could live my whole life beneath
your mud-yellow spell

We're all standing on the edge
of the same cliff

+++

Crimson songs in the hazy air, crimson
air like paprika in the songs

Fashioning reeds to blow the pigment onto walls
as they undulate and bend inward

Genius perspective
such that the paintings ripple as though glimpsed
underwater

Outliving the race of horses, aurochs, wild
boar

Outlasting erasure

THE TRANSIENCE OF PRESENCE

The sky was clear and cold though snow clouds
were building to the east

Drifting from tree to tree   in hiding
I was invisible to them

      the mechanical squirrel
      placed in the treetops

      unmoving below
      the faux fox in waiting mode

The squirrel that appeared to worry   target of slingshots
nest a mess   tree struck by lightning more than once

Intent on feeding her kit-like kits the fox
high-stepped forward in velvet boots

The squirrel leapt higher
      facsimile fur and rodent brain
      near-perfect

I reduced my breathing   stood in shadow

Remarkably like a fox   the fox nose raised to overhead trail
circled a fallen pine   snow in elaborate drifts

Near dusk   a perilous time when civilization pauses
easily undermined   animals extincted

Headfirst the squirrel-thing descended
                              scrabbling through ice for a cache

Along a frozen river   their criss-crossed prints ahead of me
I came to the scattered once-impeccable gadgetry and wiring

A scruffy grey overcoat trampled and torn
      a larger one nearby golden-red and gleaming

WINTER SOLSTICE

Darkness and forest   Cold, ice underfoot, a piercing feeling
          that I might not arrive

     The moons of Jupiter
          Io, Ganymede, Callisto, Europa, decades' worth of lesser ones
               are hidden by clouds

                    but I feel them

Fragile as old goldenrod, a light snow laces the fields

Which tree tonight
     by ice, wind, or heartbreak
will end its endless upward liftingness

                    Which tree

PREDICTION SNOW

I am writing this *slant* because if I name the missing snow
if I speak aloud or dream the soft delirious desire for it
even dare to whisper its sibilances
to surrender utterly to it as it descends from aloft
where it is gathered and stored and saved for later
now is later—do you see

We are in the later

The misplaced snow keeps coming
swirling breathing crystallizing dropletting—elsewhere
Dear permafrost I am face down on top of you I am begging you
I wait for the new downfalling
gyration of each flake a small sound a humming a tiny jostling murmur
just beyond my hearing in the huge breath-held silence
the transformation the trans the form the a ah aah
all way to the n—wait for it

We are late

DEPTH MODEL OF THE SELF AS EFT

An eft, incandescent orange with darker orange spots,
indescribably itself, crawls across the forest path

toward the sheltering leaves and flowers of a woodland violet.
It enters the Camino del Sueño—or is this me, a member

of the species that has carelessly contributed to the near-extinction
of newts and their erstwhile friends and relatives

long before a marvellous and monstrous black donut hole
re-envelops the foreseeable and beyond.

Among the violets I find moisture and shade—
there is iNaturalist and my photo now added to the cloud,

distribution of myself and kin where once there
were pristine water bodies and native insects. As my CNS

is now deranged, incapable of envisioning the self
as adult newt with the attendant responsibilities of

aquatic mating, offspring production and the like,
I note in my journal we need to create a pool immediately

because after leaving the shelter of the violets
we are bound to seek the aquatic over the terrestrial

as our life cycle requires, and no newt on earth
can survive without its divine pool, vernal or otherwise,

preferably surrounded by beech, maples, oaks,
and ash, unless you deem essential the addition

of certain microscopic organisms, dear amphibious spirit,
with which to succour your acolytes—

+++

Our Camino del Sueño is now a tectonic fault. As we awaken
in the west having fallen asleep in the east, continental drift

is triggered. Before the delicate instruments invented to measure
such large-scale motion, we were the ones who most longed for

a pathway to the water. Now with the shimmering moon
heretofore thought to be solely a Hollywood invention

beneath which untold numbers of persons, and my friend,
are calmly shooting their bodies full of fentanyl

and other horrific substances, I awake a full-bodied
if slightly careworn human without substance or solution,

aghast, overlooking a vast corrupted inland sea,
nowhere on earth to lay my or my beloved friend's heads.

PARTIAL CLOUD

The deep brain insists: adaptation
carries one only so far. Thus

only behind aquarium glass does the
octopus cease dreaming, the neon-blue

stingray circumnavigate the central atrium,
a doggedness bordering on obsession.

Should you mourn the plight
of black cherry trees, their piteous decline

for luxurious cabinetry, consider instead
the shrinking Arctic Circle, the death

of thousands of years of ice. I was inside
the roundabout and you were outside.

We waved and called.
On the side of the Coit Tower

where the Golden Gate Bridge dominates the skyline
all the windows are locked.

PEONY

There is too much orange—
the eft I cradle, salmon on whole wheat,
the sitter's nail polish

>   This morning my brain is programmed
>   to unfold its peony

I turn off the house lights
recite my self-help list

>   how the scent disrupts the brand newness
>   of mid-May air

>   petals in my vesicles, vaulting the synaptic
>   clefts

So quiet in the house
the sound of a fox swishing through grass on black toes
is amplified

Sharp snap could be a twig
but later I discover

>   a vole's velveteen jacket
>   flung into the undergrowth

bright lantern of the delicate face
snuffed

      neurotransmitters
      texting from the peony seeds

THE ARCHIVE OF LIMINAL RHETORICAL THOUGHT

My clothes are compilations of vinyl records. Many are 78s; several
still spin.

Underexploited, the metaphysics of garments: an occasion for weeping.

Among petals of clouds, tapioca, hospital sheets, I cannot locate my
   commodities.

At intervals there is a tenderness in my condition.

Which is more like a chandelier, a dog or a daydream?

Every banality has an edge; concrete is both brutal and serene.

An urban planner dictates gravel here, sidewalk there, and the
   voluptuous shade of a downtown tree vanishes.

With it, the former sky. The sky does not perceive its formerness. It
   beats the sidewalk blue. Clouds imagine their future as water drops.

I disappear into graffiti, outside chronology.

Moving like the force that opens morning glories.

THE THEN

I have stood under the great plane trees.

I have run beneath the stone aqueducts that carried water to Rome.

I've won the lottery a dozen times

and look where it's gotten me:
I can barely distinguish your tattooed back from the wallpaper.

+++

Anything that shines in the undergrowth or in the overhead

can return me to the then.

When I was hastily assembled from snow, rain, and sleet.

How extraordinary was the wind.

+++

Now I fall in love with several people
at the same time,

study circular statistics, the trajectories of raindrops,
the real lives of lawn chairs.

+++

When I visit the doctor I ask why she's holding her breath
when it's mine she's measuring.

Why here the clocks are kept behind bars.

Why the backdrop keeps disappearing.

If I am held up to the light will there be anything there.

A ROLLER COASTER, A HIT, A PINT-SIZED DEVIL MACHINE, SOME DARK CHOCOLATE

From the mud road emanated a swirl
of yellow butterflies

Then I remembered to forget the small ugly town
where I was born and raised

whose butterflies had gone missing   whose circus tent
was torn down

There were children in the trees   then flying
through the air

At the end of the road a flock
of green parakeets vaulted heavenward

All I needed was one golden fix
to be good until afternoon   Whatever it takes

A man with a wooden wheelbarrow transported his son
everywhere   tenderly   amidst rows of coconut palms and yucca

The dandelion queen for a day
was someone I grew up with

Here a soccer game sucks all the light
from a room

The metal roofs bang hard   whap whap   in a wind
that pushes itself along the road up from the iron green river

The ice cream wagon sounds its old rubber
klaxon   dogs fly through the air

along with the children on Mango Moon nights
chickens on a steady diet of popcorn Styrofoam

I need right now a roller coaster   a hit   a pint-size
devil machine   some dark chocolate

The middle-aged man still pushing his son
years later between lime green and sky blue

+++

Stand back   I'm taking on sadness in a kick-boxing
contest   aiming to break it open tonight   every night

Please be my high diving board   I want to emerge from
my past tense and feel real

Blue songs in the clouds   blue clouds in the songs

If my mouth is graphite   my throat is an alphabet
and my lips like to lip-sync everything they've heard

The ruins of family run backward
petrified inside a tree of life and death

pulling up the dregs of summer rain from the stone aquifer
and quickly   quickly now

the leaves unfurl   releasing us and O2   with
or without those sticky ribbons of love

+++

I stole from you a noun
hijacked a verb

I declared I'm mostly female   a peony
in the mouth of spring   too late

I've constructed a gorgeous building equal to or better than
any one of Gehry's   made from my and Lou Reed's

cross-dressing days   Be careful in the large
incarceration space of America   be very careful

STUDY IN BLUE-GREY

I've seen you scramble through Union Square,
slide sideways into the Emergency Happiness Store.

Under certain conditions I might accompany you to your hotel.
(Do not even contemplate the princess costume.)

You should sashay out in your eye patch, sing the prelude to "Always
    Crashing in the Same Car."

When you spot a migratory terrapin attempting to cross Broadway at
    39th, give it a hand.

I seek the largest ripe peach from all-night groceries,
return with identical pairs of ballet shoes, overconfident in my
Manhattan slang.

Old grief in my dreams becomes splashes of blue-grey
that scale the inner atrium wall of your hotel
and intensify.

That blue is the surface of the sky, peeling.

FIVE AND A HALF

I am seasick in the orphanage
that is not by the sea. I have a tiny bell
tied to a shoe,
a sharkskin shoelace left behind.
I am one; they are many.
I am five and a half
years old, no naps left to call upon
in case of danger, no lucky star I should
thank. Landlocked cereal
and no more milk
could be my founding mother.

L'AVENIR

The film of your life flashes you back
to a place and time you suppress—
How insufferable you were, teenaged,
presenting your most splintered self,

unwilling guardian of family secrets.
How thrilling advanced geometry, seen
from the outside! And theoretical physics,
its allure to a certain high school sub-cult

you willed your frontal cortex to get out in front of ...
After the ninth boy break-up, your dark hair
chopped—badly—from one day to the next. A clean break,
his sister giggled under her breath. Stealing his
hockey skates was your short path to local stardom, your revenge,

though his helmet hid your hacked hair for most of the season.
A long-winded skid on a slippery secondary,
you were searching sky for the rainbow's double,
event horizon you could claim
as one who delivered on her brags and promises.

Down that emptied-out highway, no one to witness
your dad's car gone wrong, soft belly-landing
in the devil's paintbrush-speckled meadow,
your confession a week later, steering wheel and your neck
in want of adjustment.

It was only the first leg of summer,
you were up to no good,
edging toward the ranks of runaways,
in between schools, in between small eastern towns—
Saint-Camille, Danville, L'Avenir.

i.m. Niki Smyth

ETHICS, WITNESS, SURRENDER, DILEMMA, DISTRACTION, SLEEP DEPRIVATION

The insanity of one day keeps expanding into twilight,
unable to rest, then inhales the vast dark (beyond twilight)
that will make it whole.

Bits of black gathered by the last visible branches—
that tree lifted above all others
will be struck down first.

A sound increasing in immensity, high pitched, indescribable,
as from a long buried musical instrument
being carried to the surface of the earth.

I step into it, up it whips through the soles of my shoes,
into my teeth and jaw,
my neck, the crown

of my head that might blossom
like the tree was blossoming
a day in early May.

I could be the yellow jackets
competing over windfall apples
their strangely six-sided seeing, in altered colours.

+++

Tag end of February, so tired on my drive home I believe full moonrise
is sunset, though I wonder
at the swaths of chill,

mercuric light, as thousands of deep-sea creatures erupt
from the trench
opening just beside

my small blue car. Another disequilibrium. Farther off, the two
moons of Pluto
tighten their orbits

and a meteor comes to grief over Russia, changing the fortune
of one small city from bad to good.
The past

increasingly remote. Nearby, birch trees flare
on the moss-freckled hill
adjacent to the unexpected meltwater.

+++

Now that my father has been dead seven times seven years
I have unrolled the rug
he shipped home,

the Turkish rug that was always underfoot, and rolled
myself up in it,
beginning precisely

(he was a mathematician) at one corner—
all these years
I've been smouldering.

AFTER-IMAGE

For a long time she saw the after-image

Flakes would drift across a particular scene
or wavering green-grey stripes would scroll up and down
an empty wall

These things were both peripheral and embedded

A red cloud emanating as a blood orange
was bitten into

+++

In the maize field her hair was lifted straight up

      Her blue dress down about her knees

One finger pointing toward the sky

+++

Did the volcano erupt last night

      A crow hops back and forth   It was
the propane tank
     again

Violet-sided Popo, with a snow cone top

It's feast or famine out there

+ + +

What would she have made of this poinsettia tree

        Not belonging here but aching to

Reservoir of water, reservoir of sky

       The moon poles across the river

The undifferentiated dark is all around us   angels too

Very tall with silvery wings high as treetops

        Feel the wind when they alight on the barn roof
shocking the bejesus out of the rooster

If they descend further onto the moonlight-slicked grass

Not speaking in angel tongues   assessing us

How do you feel   Would you ever   Was she with you

Was that when she began her slide

       Her words became feathered   or was that her arms

Did she thereafter aspire   Was her confidence set aside

Did you dream of their hair flickering

Are you circling the abyss   Was she

I am prepared to be extinguished by the night   Are you

The startle of popsicle-red bougainvillea, banana-leaf mural
    on an apartment building shadowed by a huge palm tree

Listening to "Una noche en Villa Fontana"   hecho en Mexico

"El Pájaro Azul," "Oración Caribe," "Pasión," "Peregrino de Amor"

Time is squared   Everywhere is temporary

Hot light pouring through the bedroom window

Tell me your earliest memory

+++

During the scant time between our births   me and my brother

Both grandfathers died and one grandmother
came to live with us   then three younger sisters

This being the order of external events

Internal ones   beyond our grasp

TWENTY-THREE

There is only time recorded before the year, then a gap,
don't mind the gap, then

after. And if time, that stopped for that whole year,
derives from molecules

of cosmic dust hastily assembled as black holes that were instantly
reassembled into a series of stills, I was the last to know.

After the gateway for my mother's spirit opened,
daily I sat in a folding chair with an unobstructed view of the sea.

I waited. Flocks of time flew overhead low and dark,
creating a symphony atonal yet mighty; my response to her death

went on and on. Ever since the white skunk visited,
after a lengthy walk along the pebble beach,

the river of musical time resumed, swooping
past the dog star. Dust was raised, digital time began. *Hello 24.*

JUNG'S GREEN WAVES OF CONSCIOUSNESS

The green is not a colour she has seen in her life. It is the green of
    a few. Eye-filling. It peaks in a fluorescent crescendo. Everything
    afterward

is down a hill. Her numbness, her abraded skin. Peripheral vision
    awash.
The man who rescues her leery and weary. Who plies her with blankets,

kindles a fire. Who will not discuss the wave's possible intentions.
If she is hauling a huge load, the man gestures, she can put it down

over there in that meadow. There will be a small house ahead, a serape
across the doorway and a leftover person from a war sleeping inside.

A lantern nearby and a horse, out back, will be waiting for her to ride it
    across the beach
to the time before the wave.

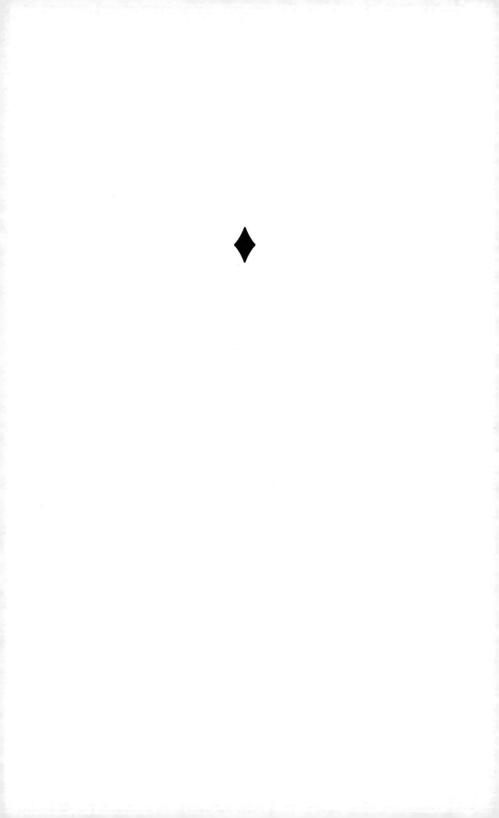

TO REMEMBER WHAT NEVER EXISTED: LAMENT AND LYRIC FOR CLARICE LISPECTOR

1

The mineral black door of night slides open, Clarice,
    you in sole possession
    of the atoms of time.
As a child in Recife, you were the chargé d'affaires
    of leaf-cutting ants, spiked and lacquered like armoured
    samurai—death to leaves and blossoms.
One after another they followed a green scent on the wind
into sugar cane fields where you crouched,
    dressed for Carnival as a rose.

2

Moonlight on your left.
You wonder if you were born a turtle.
When you sail through the Portuguese language
       you leave a wake.
Each word fishing for something not a word.
That initial rustle, a heart beating under the earth.

3

You, in Rio, invented weekly newspaper columns,
favoured, in turn, an arsonist, a friend of roosters,
        a finder of lost shoes.

You insisted é was *the* essential verb in Portuguese, captivated
        by its *is*-ness, fervent for the *this*.
        What I tell you is never what I tell you
        but something else.

Charles Babbage's *Ninth Bridgewater Treatise* averred
        ...pulsations of the air, once set in motion by the human voice,
        cease not to exist ...

Therefore your electrons, Clarice, have not ceased their momentum
any more than have this morning's goldfinches, relieving
the sunflowers of their black-hulled seeds.

4

Life presses in; objects emanate an odour of steel.
The Dalí clocks have stopped and a hoarse chime
slides down the wall. So many moons in the sky!
You say: And what about the room? Where would it store all that light
when it goes to sleep?

5

Today there's a chill in the yellow linoleum.
Fringed orchids spring up in your stream bed,
      rain scribbles new sentences in gravel and sand.
      You can't translate this language; you're streambed illiterate.
The grasses stand and look at the sky but you lie down.

6

The dark of complete darkness—not one hint of light will be tolerated.
　　The pressure, temperature, and humidity are painstakingly
　　adjusted to favour some life forms over others: not the orchids,
born already art, nor the water-loving arums.
　　It will keep getting hotter. You will never meet me
　　in the rooftop park of that iconic building
as arranged. The rivers will take their shimmer underground
　　and forego resurfacing.

7

Yes, you trapped lightning in a jar—and it is blue.
    You brought a lily, and it is now the hour of the star.
Into your arms and legs, you have carved tiny hearts, each
with its own arrow. You live on favela time. [   ]
    The lustre has fled from the soil,
    the colour of the world dimmer here
than there. In your chest, a lukewarm sensation. Do you feel
the voluptuousness
    of the rain; do you hand over
    the few grams of your soul in silence?
All your beauty turning on a compass rose.

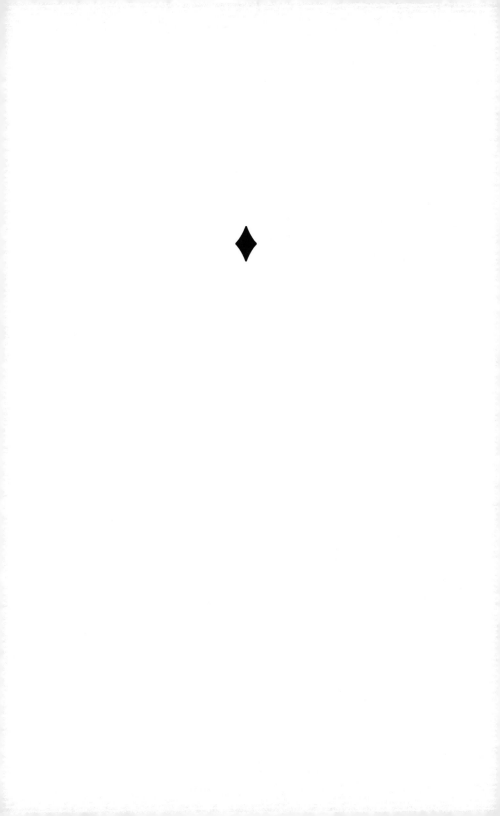

ONE MORNING IN THE LIFE OF FOG

I who have often imagined myself as an irrational number
I who can disappear by closing my eyes

I would like to know the absolute value of anything
in case I am asked

In the curious hour before daylight breaks open
I walk into a bank of fog

      where I can practice being a decimal point
      a fraction of

I would like to know how a falling cloud
feels, on descent, briefly touching down

      onto the back of a swan asleep on a pond
      beading on her feather gown, temporary

      suspended between water and air
      oxygen discarding then calling back its hydrogens

      now lifting away, leaving below feathers, swan, pond
        curve
            of
               blue

AI WEIWEI'S RAT

Designed for the Qianlong Emperor, cast during what we call
the eighteenth century, I was weighty, a metre high,
zodiacal, one of twelve animal spirits of the water clock

fountain. In front of the Haiyan Tang, atop stone
I balanced, open-mouthed. Once a day
water hit my bronze throat and I sang.

Listened to the rustle of my kin in the choked storerooms,
in the granaries, while injunctions and susurrations of servants
stirred twilight. Rose when occasion required,

and bowed lower than the lowest grasses.

+++

Heeding rumours of British and French burning and looting,
the keyholder of the Library of the Four Seasons
in peau de soie robes hastily gathered treasures

to spirit away. Pried from the Emperor's minor throne
a pearl the size of a hazelnut
rolled to a standstill nearby.   *Shhhhhhhhhhhh.*

Je ne suis pas une perle! Je ne suis pas une perle!
she chanted, eyes squeezed shut.

+++

I was post-empire, an opium addict, relieved at being first
of seven survivors, merely looted and uprooted with Rabbit
to the City of Lights, not pitched

into the Vast Empty Clear Mirror alongside Dragon, Rooster,
Snake, Goat, and Dog. They never surfaced.
In those concentric Paris suburbs each fake-silver spray-painted

assault on my ears I withstood unflinchingly. Rabbit
took to hip hop. Having evaded discovery, tucked into my cheek,
Pearl fell in love. It was springtime in Paris.

BOX CAR

That locomotive from 1935—
the fronts of the rods, the backs of the pistons, only three wheels!

On bended knee we beseech the tanker car: offload
your petroleum, lead a leaner, cleaner life.

Family with extended visas at the RR crossing, late
to transport toad with smashed fibula to renowned clinic.

In watermelon, VIA Rail flags are implanted. Sir Fleming,
do not despair, we are nearly there (where?) with
our discounted boxes of penicillin. Viva VIA! Viva VIA!

Salamanders uncouple in the yards to forestall
the company plan of open marriage.

Scotch-taped to the tracks are our three pennies. The skinny
unrescued heroine fumes.

Sometimes the beam of a motorcycle is the headlamp of a train.

Sometimes the headlamp stutters: boxcar box car box   car   box

THE OLD STOCK EXCHANGE TRADING ROOM

Everywhere you go, the music of Lollapalooza precedes you.

No stakeholders in Riverdale or Fuller Park.

Many doors along Michigan Avenue's Magnificent Mile; none open to you.

Who will know your ambitions?

Abakanowicz' headless, armless torsos and their huge feet follow you through the urban maze, always in a blues spotlight.

Here you are free to be at the frayed margins of yourself.

Crisscrossing the Chicago River you use a different bridge each day and begin to identify as a feminist lake-going vessel.

Once before you lifted a boulder up into a tree.

You concoct a daring plan to remove the first letter of a name on a certain tower but are foiled by a policeman riding a horse through your safety net.

AUTUMN TROUT

To be trout   fishing in America
Or merely an autumn trout circling the imagination of Anne Carson
In my nightmares   I am shellacked   mounted on a plaque
Speckled, spackled   my fins rub against plaster

I also identify with flies listening on walls   and those cast
upon the unsteady surface

of mountain streams   known only to a handful of cognoscenti
Flies tied intricately   by those with nimble fingers
who ransack for primaries the British Museum of Natural History
Drawers filled with row upon row   shelf life unknown
Common loon   peacock   quetzal   cardinal
   white-throated sparrow
For a trout be so bestowed with feathers
the way I envision Margot Fonteyn   in Lac des Cygnes
   white and sleek

But I am a fish   immobile beneath iridescent scales
   having misspent
young trout days hidden in deep winter pools   my fins
   a natural wonder
like a peninsula   to an islander

If I transform into an octopus
I could escape from my plaque   in seconds flat
   having camouflaged myself
as wall plaster   eased myself down   out the window
into an earlier poem

LATE VIEW OF THE ANTHROPOCENE

There's North Carolina
where I no longer go,
and Mississippi.

Re: design
one hat
is all she wanted. I wake

all the objects in my room:
stones from Newfoundland,
Nigerian goat bone.

She comes in shock waves.
Steps across the threshold
with a gravitas

that slams me through
the window.
I am slow connecting the dots.

She's convinced the single rifle shot
that quirks the avalanche
is urban myth. Artificial light

anomalous in the sunbeamed room.
I claim particle physics.
She parts the Grand Canyon;

I fling open doors of the continent—
dry and sandy on the outside,
molten within.

Some cars whizz by
by the hundreds, avoid
going home. Others linger at storefronts,

bars, fire halls—drivers
velcroed by memory
to their seats. They are

unhinged, she says, in denial.
We take the trail
left here.

IF IT TUMBLES DOWN

Battling neither-here-nor-there fatigue
in brilliant yellow darkness.
The tiniest sounds of fracture—
all eighths disappear from the Inch River.

Tomorrow the lights go out, the bone
xylophone comes into its own.
Albeit traumatized,
we'll stroke the thing that hides

from the mouths of electrical eels,
place our ears closer to clouds.
Echo, for instance, the sound of water
fleeing down stairs of grass.

CASA MILÀ, BARCELONA

The aliveness of the rooftop with atavistic
chimneys is muted by linked walkways, fences,
and streams of tourists. Even so, we are blown away—
wind, water, earth, fire, one for every corner

of the world. Of these elements, I sometimes identify
with fire, perhaps to counterbalance my water self,
the self enamoured of in-between and thresholds,
of half here and half nowhere. Where the kingfisher

dives in flames into water. I am not drawn to edges;
they are drawn to me. The geometry of the hundreds
of catenary arches is vertebral and visceral. I feel the breath
of a gargantuan organism inhaling me and the building,

all the scale models of La Pedrera splintering—but then
I am outside on Carrer de Provença, and light is singing, ping-
ping, wave upon wave, building the day into
another structure, one that more or less resembles

my life. And if there are chimneys fantastic
and dream-ridden, embedded with ceramic fragments,
and a wildly tilting, undulating facade in my inner life,
that landscape is hidden from the eyes of the world.

PART STAR, PART VENOM, PART BONE, PART MICROPLASTIC

Are roses your company-keepers

Me, I have a love-hate relationship with reds and pinks

    She believed he was rain blue on the inside

She marches to her own drum
                      playing a flute

    If water weren't wet, what would it be

The sound around here is peppered with black-and-white silences

When she puts her eye to a mirror, she sees
    herself with a ferocious unsparing clarity

+++

How are your BTUS

Fear of taking precipitous action, what's that called

    Purple side up, violet side down

What range of decibels do you lay claim to

That hat is fake, I can always tell
a fake hat

I don't really know why that hornet has taken
such a brazen dislike to me

Her rainy-day fund consists of two marigolds
and a peach tree

I've found that arguing with a snapping turtle
is unlikely to have a positive outcome

If you recall the password to that oak tree door
I'd appreciate hearing it

One little acorn was all she knew

+++

He could bake a cherry pie with or without the cherries

If you dream of snails there is a slow burn in your future

I'll bet you don't eat salamander eggs much
do you

Now she thinks is a good time to visit her squirrel's grave
up on the hill

One dream, two fantasies, three nightmares

    The treacherous woman and her saintly husband
        moved in down the road

When he hung up his boxing gloves a hush
fell over the land

The camel-riding visitor arrived unexpectedly last week

    I just love to bingo all day on a holiday weekend

Kissing a frog could have unforeseen consequences

How far are you willing to go to see the world's
    smallest dream hole

    The weather vane sends messages pretty regularly to my
      grandfather
through the air vents

        I'm living in twilight, how about you

Tell me your story, I'll tell you someone else's

+++

A saxophone solo late in the night deepens from black
        to ultraviolet

If you hear it, follow the sound wherever it takes you

+++

We were greatly swayed in our thinking
            by the rabbit sketched on the full moon's face

        Her tattoos were unexpected—hundreds of ants climbing up and
            down
arms and legs

            I wondered what trail they are following

I said quietly, *The ants are here now*   *They are your friend*
        Don't be afraid
        of anything

+++

                    Here's my mother again
                    for a visit

                    One of us cross-legged on a cloud
                    I don't think it's me

Hi Mom, I say
cheerfully
You're looking
a little more transparent
these days

Everything OK?

The generator failed again
and your father is off dragging clouds
from one vision to another

I want to go home
she says

But Mom, I think
you are home

(In my family I'm known as the tactful one

A million kilos of loneliness drop onto
my shoulders

I stay upright   trying hard

Do the right thing
I think that's what she says
by way of goodbye

+++

Right now, right here, I'm trying hard to inhabit the month of June

     Seems to be extra-slippery this year

     If raised non-Catholic do you automatically
carry a few grams less guilt

If I were wandering lonely as a cloud

If you were too

Maybe we could meet somewhere off-planet and out of range
     to consider our situation

If I ever get out of here

If she is ever restored to her former glory

If not, not

The flight attendant assured me
    that saying the Lord's Prayer 3x daily
        in every school

    would prevent all mass shootings in America

I don't buy it

We humans   part star, part venom   part bone, part microplastic

What percent star are you

        Is the worst over yet

It's never over

    It goes like this   until it doesn't

THE RED OAK

You were here when we moved
to Massachusetts, on the north slope
distant from other oaks, though you tolerate

the singing aspen for its light, complex notes,
the stately form of the white pine—
I sit nearby, or, ear pressed

against your bark, listen for the wild thrumming
of the world. Now I know your roots
compose intricate signals to transmit

to their neighbours, but not to me—
it should be calming
to be so unnecessary.

In the fall, musky blood-red, your leaves
adorn the few twigs
the squirrels leave attached.

Each morning a rain of branches,
each afternoon a wind descends
gently shaking you up and down—

Come with me, come away with me.

How will I find you, in the afterlife
of trees, when I am wandering from
ridgetop to ridgetop, calling your name?

FIRST TO FLOWER

I have heard you murmuring
about the perennial bed where I dwell
nearly crushed by soil, rock, and snow

As though this life of mine that is endless
were a wonder—
perhaps I am the apex of all your striving

For me this existence is a form of torment:
unable to awaken fully, in the feral darkness
fearful of rodents, defenseless

Only when the ice melts do I recall
my ancestry: Theophrastus named me
white violet, first to appear

despite chill wind and fitful light
near the dwarf conifer and the glinting boulder
beneath dog-eared snow patches

I stir. My greenery is
a colour
not yet of this world—

Albeit flowering face down as though in obeisance
to you who buried me here
I enjoy my modest share of admiration

from the moths that come calling
the small ones
no one cares to name

You recall my existence for a few scant days—
is it fair that I should return to obscurity
while you carry on, sunlit and aloof?

IRONWEED

There is something in you of an iron-sided steamship
an architecture of unpliable stems, toothed
leaves, a crow's nest of disk flowers

a pile of deep violet slippers
uplifted on junkyard stilts

stiff-kneed, towering overhead
as though dredged from some scrap-iron seabed

and winched roots-first into place
overrunning meadows and pastures

obdurate perennials, late-summer bloomers

witnesses to night-long astonishment
as the Perseids brilliantine their long hair and flare
and the stars stutter, waking from a long dream
of falling

LATE SUMMER

Hazy day in August

Crow acrobatics and poplar leaves twitching

    Trees lean in to catch grass thoughts

A light breeze, let the smooth side ride

    If I concentrate, a rose blooms inside a neuron

New shade of rouge then a sensual scent

    Presto a garden on the inside looking out

+++

Something in the woods is making quite a racket

Somewhere in a house legs twitch in a fugue state

    What do I love? A tree frog on the window sill, green
        river heron, muskrat, beaver lodge in the backwater

Sleep slips out between venetian blinds

Dishwasher foam on the shores of the kitchen floor

Into the yard floats the red of a local barn

Sparking the gorget of the ruby-throat

I'm still here, just off the turnpike between Stockbridge and Boston

Neighbours mow their lawns, we uproot our C4 grasses

A smokescreen appears or is that fine ash blown in
from West Coast fires
covering the world or was that a can of paint

One day can replicate another or not

+++

In a garbage pail our friend traps porcupines, releases them
in the next county

Woods filled with lost porcupines munching through the night

Twin black-and-white dogs live down the road, coyotes up on the hill

+++

We five kids used to hide beneath the dining-room table

Worrying the shoes of our parents and grandparents

Now fog collects there, asking, is it safe?

Deer hunker in the old apple orchard, is it safe?

Carpenter ants explore the deck and disappear into crevasses

    Open a door into morning and you're sucked right into the afterlife

A gooseneck lamp but no geese on the lawn
   queuing for the southern leg

    I sink into a sea of thyme and bumblebees each time
      I step off the deck

Here comes the next wave

Here comes the light of ironweed and goldenrod

    No one notices I have been off-line for days

+++

If you stand still long enough the trees forget you exist and draw nearer

    The day exits first and holds open the door

I concentrate on dreaming of watching myself walking away

Instead I get him hiking glaciers near the border

Dehydrated, I awake and fill a thermos of water to take to him

+++

The sun around here expects a rental fee

The delinquent suffer excess clouds, larger hail, the biggest horseflies

A model society: four species of lichen on a single rock

    There are always ferns

At the front edge of the storm the sky fills with nighthawks

Ozone like an alcohol buzz

    From the second floor it's easy to fly out a window

+++

Time for the rain

Time for the moss count

Watch the Talking Heads on late night TV and jog around the studio,
    paint brush in hand

Graffiti on the run

    A synergism of black-eyed Susans and hawkweed, bear
      in the cherry tree

No sound but the bubbles in the fish tank

Or is it the Gulf Stream
    reversing course in the middle of the yard

Jellyfish on the roof

    Sideways is one way to go

Do the laundry, slide into the slipstream

Don't forget to count the rings of Saturn
    before you turn off the moon

NOTES

An eft is the juvenile land-dwelling stage of the eastern red-spotted newt, *Notophthalmus viridescens*, common in the northeastern region of North America. It makes two appearances: in "Depth Model of the Self as Eft" and nearby in "Peony."

"Partial Cloud": From the windows of the Coit Tower in San Francisco, the Golden Gate Bridge, a known location for those contemplating suicide, is visible. The locked windows are an effort to prevent suicide from this landmark.

"The Archive of Liminal Rhetorical Thought" is for Maria Anice Sallum.

"A Roller Coaster, A Hit, A Pint-Sized Devil Machine, Some Dark Chocolate": The phrase, "... a peony/in the mouth of spring, too late," was borrowed and altered from Ocean Vuong.

"Study in Blue-Grey" quotes the title of the song, "Always Crashing in the Same Car," by David Bowie, 1977. It also mentions The Emergency Happiness Store, which may still exist where I first saw it, in the town of Fish Hoek, outside Cape Town, South Africa.

"After-Image": Popo is an affectionate nickname for the major volcano Popocatepetl in the Valley of Mexico. At times when the air is clear it is visible in the City of Mexico.

Charles Babbage (1791–1871) was a brilliant English computer pioneer. The original text of *The Ninth Bridgewater Treatise* was published in 1837 (London: John Murray), and includes some curious ideas, e.g., that sounds and utterances from human voices never entirely dissipate.

Sources for "To Remember What Never Existed: Lament and Lyric for Clarice Lispector" include:

Lispector, C. 1972. *Family Ties*. Trans. Pontiero, G. University of Texas Press, Austin.

Lispector, C. 1989. *Soulstorm*. Trans. Levitin, A. New Directions Books, NY.

Lispector, C. 1990. *Near to the Wild Heart*. Trans. Pontiero, G. New Directions Books, NY.

Lispector, C. 1986. *The Hour of the Star*. Trans. Pontiero, G. Carcanet Press, Manchester.

Lispector, C. 1989. *The Stream of Life*. Trans. Lowe, E. and Fitz, E. University of Minnesota Press, Minneapolis.

Lispector, C. 1996. *Selected Crônicas*. Trans. Pontiero, G. New Directions Books, NY.

Lispector, C. 2015. *The Complete Stories*. Trans. Dodson, K., ed. Moser, B. New Directions Books, NY.

In 2010 artist Ai Weiwei recreated the twelve bronze animals of the Chinese zodiac that had been an integral part of a water clock fountain (AKA clepsydra) at the Yuanming Yuan (Old Summer Palace) in Beijing. They were originally commissioned by the Qianlong Emperor during the Qing Dynasty and are thought to have been designed and cast around 1750 by Giuseppe Castiglione and another Jesuit living at the Emperor's court. Some (possibly seven) were looted during the Second Opium War in 1860 and had various fates: several are still unaccounted for. The narrator in "Ai Weiwei's Rat" is the original bronze rat that may have spent some years at the Chinese Museum in the Palace of Fontainebleau, and subsequently as part of Yves St. Laurent's private art collection.

Lollapalooza is an annual music festival that moves around various American cities. In "The Old Stock Exchange Trading Room," the venue was Chicago. Sculptures by Polish sculptor Magdalena Abakanowicz defy description. Go to Grant Park in Chicago and walk among them.

In "Autumn Trout," the first line refers to the novel *Trout Fishing in America*, 1967, Four Seasons Foundation, by American writer Richard Brautigan (1935–1984).

A Grecian philosopher in the Peripatetic school, designated by Aristotle as his successor, Theophrastus (371–c. 287 BC) named, described and wrote major botanical treatises on many plants, among other writings. The flower envoiced in "First to Flower" is proud to have been designated 'white violet' initially by Theophrastus, even though that common name for this species (presumed *Galanthus nivalis,* based on geographic distribution) has been supplanted by 'snowdrop.'

ACKNOWLEDGEMENTS

I want to acknowledge that, here in Great Barrington, western Massachusetts, I am standing on the traditional lands of the Mohican People, and honour with gratitude the land itself and the people who have stewarded it throughout the generations. Great Barrington is also the birthplace of the pioneering civil rights proponent and activist, W.E.B. Du Bois (1868–1963).

I wish to warmly thank all the editors of the following journals for publishing poems from this book, some as earlier versions:

Arc: "Late View of the Anthropocene," "L'Avenir"

CV2: "If It Tumbles Down," "To Remember What Never Existed: Lament and Lyric for Clarice Lispector"

Fiddlehead: "Ethics, Witness, Surrender, Dilemma, Distraction, Sleep Deprivation," "Partial Cloud," "Ai Weiwei's Rat," "Box Car," "Study in Blue-Grey," "The Archive of Liminal Rhetorical Thought," "The Then," "Autumn Trout," "Late Summer"

Panorama: The Journal for Travel, Place and Nature (UK): Excerpts of "A Roller Coaster, A Hit, A Pint-Sized Devil Machine, Some Dark Chocolate," After-Image," "Part Star, Part Venom, Part Bone, Part Microplastic," https://panoramajournal.org/issues/issue-8-space/

PRISM international: "The Old Stock Exchange Trading Room"

The Antigonish Review: "Jung's Green Waves of Consciousness"

The Malahat Review: "Five and a Half," "Peony"

The Puritan: "Ironweed"

"Partial Cloud" was featured on *The Fiddlehead* website from January through March, 2017.

"Peony" was the subject of an interview, "A Peony to Pique the Senses: Chloe Hogan-Weihmann in Conversation with Jan Conn," in *The Malahat Review*: https://web.uvic.ca/malahat/interviews/conn_interview2.html

"Prediction Snow" was exhibited at Jardins des Métis, Quebec, in the fall of 2022 and on IG as part of the collaborative project, "Four Seasons," by Mark Raynes Roberts. With special thanks to Mark for his support of my poems and paintings, particularly his IG "Creation in Isolation" project of 2020–2021.

"Prediction Snow" was published online as part of the abstract, "The Language of Biology," in *Re-visioning Ecology and Evolution – how can creative writing connect and reveal scientific truths,* Session 1149075, organized by Madhur Anand, University of Guelph, for the joint Ecological Society of America/Canadian Society of Ecology and Evolution meeting, held in Montreal, August 14–19, 2022.

"The Transience of Presence," "Prediction Snow," "Depth Model of the Self as Eft," and "Peony" were recorded as part of the Virtual

STEM Poetry Reading Series, SUNY Farmington State College on April 25, 2023. The recording is available at https://youtu.be/Ubu1vhmEKPE. My warmest thanks to Danielle Apfelbaum, Scholarly Communication Librarian at SUNY FSC, for her kind invitation to participate.

"The Transience of Presence" is forthcoming in the anthology "Tracks," ed. Jeffrey A. Lockwood, Middle Creek Press, Colorado, 2023.

"Ironweed" was a notable poem of 2023, listed in the *Best Canadian Poetry* anthology, 2023, guest ed. John Barton, series ed. Anita Lahey, Biblioasis, Windsor, Ontario. Thanks to both of you.

I am delighted to thank Sonnet L'Abbé for their extraordinary editing skills and their nuanced sensitivity of language, gender, race, and national identity. They pushed me to think more deeply about these poems, a great gift.

Deepest gratitude to the Brick Books team: Marijke Friesen for the cover design, Publisher Alayna Munce for her indefatigable enthusiasm, generous support, and outstanding copy-editing, and CFO/COO Brenda Leifso for guidance and travel organization.

I am greatly indebted to Stan Dragland (1942–2022), who was my editor at Brick Books for three previous collections of poetry (*Jaguar Rain, Botero's Beautiful Horses*, and *Edge Effects*). His kindness, humour, poetry chops, and outstanding editorial advice were always generously and open-heartedly offered; I was a very lucky recipient.

Thank you to Madhur Anand, Roo Borson, Kathline Carr, Lauren Clark, Margarita Correa, Mary di Michele, Elsa Franklin, Ross Fraser, Susan Gillis, Harvey L. Hix, Ian Letourneau, Kim Maltman, Jane Munro, Jim Nason, Jim Peters, Erin Robinsong, Lisa Rosenberg, Maria Anice Sallum, Lota Soder, and Richard Summerbell.

For Carlo and for my siblings: David R. Conn, Diane M. Conn, Jude Conn, and Susan Conn-Hood.

Jan Conn is a Canadian poet, biologist, and visual artist. She was born in southeastern Quebec and lives in western Massachusetts. Her poetry has received a CBC Literary Prize, the inaugural P.K. Page Founder's Award, and in 2016 was nominated for a Pushcart Prize. She works on the vector biology and evolution of Latin American mosquito vectors at the Wadsworth Center in Albany, NY. *Peony Vertigo* is her tenth collection of poetry.